Ins

and

Outs

of the

Forest

Rivers

Also by Nathaniel Tarn

POETRY

Avia (2008)
Recollections of Being (2004)
Selected Poems: 1950-2000 (2002)
Three Letters from the City: the St. Petersburg Poems (2001)
The Architextures (2000)
The Architextures 1-7 (1999)
A Multitude of One (editor; poems by Natasha Tarn, 1994)
Flying the Body (1993)
Caja del Río (1993)
The Army Has Announced that Body Bags... (1992)
Home One (1990)
Seeing America First (1989)
The Mothers of Matagalpa (1989)
At the Western Gates (1985)
The Desert Mothers (1984)
Weekends in Mexico (1982)
The Land Songs (1981)
Atitlán/Alashka (*Alashka* with Janet Rodney, 1979)
Birdscapes, with Seaside (1978)
The Forest: from Alashka (with Janet Rodney, 1978)
The Ground of Our Great Admiration... (with Janet Rodney, 1977)
The Microcosm (1977)
The House of Leaves (1976)
Lyrics for the Bride of God (1975)
The Persephones (1974, rewritten 2008)
Le Belle Contradizzione (translated by R. Sanesi, 1973)
Section: The Artemision (1973)
A Nowhere for Vallejo (1971)
The Silence (1969)
October (1969)
The Beautiful Contradictions (1969)
Where Babylon Ends (1969)
Selection: Penguin Modern Poets, 7 (1965)
Old Savage/Young City (1964)

TRANSLATIONS

The Penguin Neruda (1975)
The Rabinal Achi, Act 4 (1973)
Selected Poems (Neruda, 1970)
Stelae (Segalen, 1969)
Con Cuba (1969)
The Heights of Macchu Picchu (Neruda, 1966)

PROSE

The Embattled Lyric: Essays and Conversations... (2007)
Scandals in the House of Birds: Shamans and Priests on Lake Atitlán (1998)
Views from the Weaving Mountain: Selected Essays... (1991)

INS AND OUTS OF THE FOREST RIVERS

Nathaniel Tarn

A New Directions Book

Acknowledgments: The author wishes to thank the editors of the following journals in which some of these poems—sometimes in earlier versions—have appeared: *26 Magazine*, *Big Bridge*, *Conjunctions*, *Eyewear* (U.K.), *First Intensity*, *Hambone*, *Mandorla*, *New American Writing*, *The New Review of Literature*, *Notre Dame Review*, *The Poker*, *Talisman*, *Tears in the Fence* (U.K.).
An earlier version of "War Stills: Group One" was first published as "War Poems Yet Again" in *Recollections of Being* by Salt Publishing, Cambridge, U.K. in 2004. "Dying Trees" was published in a slightly different version by *Rain Taxi* as no.9 in their Brainstorm Series of chapbooks, Minneapolis, MN, 2003.

Manufactured in the United States of America
New Directions Books are printed on acid-free paper
First published as a New Directions Paperbook 1118 (NDP1118) in 2008
Published simultaneously in Canada by Penguin Books Canada Limited

Library of Congress Cataloging-in-Publication Data
Tarn, Nathaniel.
 Ins and outs of the forest rivers / Nathaniel Tarn.
    p. cm.
 ISBN 978-0-8112-1798-9 (pbk. : alk. paper)
 1. Spirituality—Poetry. 2. Iraq War, 2003—Atrocities—Poetry. 3. Forest degradation—Poetry. 4. Ecology—Poetry. 5. Human ecology—Poetry. I. Title.
 PS3570.A635I67 2008
 811'.54—dc22   2008022967

New Directions Books are published for James Laughlin
by New Directions Publishing Corporation
80 Eighth Avenue, New York, NY 10011

Contents

War Stills

Movement / North of the Java Sea

Sarawak

INS

AND

OUTS

OF THE

FOREST

RIVERS

Pursuit of the Whole & Parts

for John Olson

What is this self which realizes one night
that its whole life has only had one meaning:
the question of the relation of a whole to
whatever may be said to depend from it—
that most ancient of philosophical questions?
Because you cannot only pursue the whole,
desire it ardently your whole existence through,
the whole being meaningless without the part
and the part must be as carefully examined and expounded
as the whole. If you go for the whole alone,

what are you doing except entering a cloud
so that your task is to become ever more pure
until no shred of remembrance of any part remains with you
and the thought of any part immediately drowns into the whole,
[the thought or apprehension of the whole]—and you are
now so desperately wretched and one-sided. No, it is the
stubbornness, the innate cussedness [and stubbornness] of the part,
any part, [any part whatsoever], dropped by circumstance
into a consciousness, [birth taken in a consciousness]—
as part of a whole, you understand, you cannot,

[absolutely cannot] do without that part-enabling whole.
It is that stubbornness which links you to the moment,
to the circumstantial existence of yourself in time,
as if you were a note in music, or a bird
in a flock of birds disappearing into winter

and the moment is the only thing that you truly possess,
can ever possess, the very definition of possession
and that possession is the possession of a part, a part only,
indeed the moment, [the very moment], is nothing but a part,
and never yet of a whole. But then, [but then], you are straining,

[ever straining] for the selfish possession of that moment;
forgetful of the whole, that which you were first desiring,
the cloud that sits in the midst of your mind, [your mist],
which would swallow and make null all those parts as parts
floating around in the mind—and another kind of selfishness,
the selfishness of the light-hearted, the cloud-walker,
alone with his invisibles, his intangibles, all those angelic wings
with emptiness at the heart, without beings between them,
all those illusions, that beg for the want of parts,
his kingdom worth less than a horse, [merely a part, a part].

Except, of course, [except of course] if there were a signal,
if, in the midst of that cloud, all the parts were suddenly
beheld, [held] as if holding together, as if there was a pattern
discernable there and, yes, of course, my god, the moment,
[the moment] would then be both part and whole in one body,
waiting only on mind, [the holy mind], to weld them together,
what once upon a time was called the firefly of spirit,
before disappearing from this quest, not once and for all,
no never, alas, of course, [once and for all]—but merely
[merely] until the next moment, eons afterwards,

when whoever owns the machine stands again at the doorsill
and the astonishing beauty of the understanding is detected
and the knowledge that it is always there—however many times

you are at a loss in the world, [at a complete loss in the world],
to be returned to, in that new moment, which is also all the old,
as if this moment were ageless and could always return
with the astounding recurrence of air by the unbounded ocean.

OF THE

PERFECTED

ANGELS

COACHWHIP

In a summer sudden
seeming sewn from the flower petals
of cooling air—as if saying,
(it coming down from the stars
in the world's evening),
who is this? what is this?
do I know it? do I recognize
long ago punishment to be crushed by feet
   of no-longer natives?
       Thin pink Coachwhip slides along
straight, not curled, slithering,
though, at branches' confluence,
a woven tangle, coiled basketry, circles—
lightning pale, sunset-colored—
engulfs a bird feeding
which had not kept the sky in its favor.
       Careful steps out the house thereafter
stamping up a little dancing noise
in the absence of bells: not by *my* feet
nor by any fire of mine
shall this be hurt
or I be hurt by it—
for I have never sinned, not in the world's
morning, nor at any season,
though unforgiven still.
Yes, I recognize:
this is as far gone west as time's wave now
       into another peaceless country.

Of the Animal

for Nancy Kuhl & Richard Deming

Of what is coming, is undeflectable, is waited
on by all, is part of the general understanding—
and yet invisible "to whom it won't concern."
Of what he is alone in knowing then—and yet
can find no way to comprehend it, interpret it,
to read it as a whole into his system. Perhaps
it should be said "his systems." Of what both trees
and poems in their separate ways have referenced,
have signified most beautifully, exhaustively,
heart-wrenchingly, in youth when mind was fervent,
in tune with every way in which he's thought of it.
Of what has forced him more and more,
when hot to break the language, the syntax of
the language like a bunch of sticks, placing them
every way contrary to what pluralities expect,
nails him time after time back into expressions
that most will recognize. The recognition being
of the beast that comes toward his life, as to all
lives eventually, with eyes only for one, the one
alone standing his or her place, seeing beast only,
its all-embracing eyes. They will not speak of it,
in no way intimate, but only general, like gossip,
like truisms of the mentally deficient, normal ones,
what everyman, and everywoman too, is made of.
Yet, in the end, it cannot be avoided, had to
come forth in something like a form—that had
evaded form his whole life through: in beast,

it's said, because of all things known beast lets itself
be killed with no complaint. Thus lord of its domain.
Beast who has angel's patience, or so they say
of the perfected angels, can wait a hundred years, or
even more so now, to savor what is sacrificed.
He sees the animal, the only thing on earth
that has a soul—as "animal" will teach you—
lives with the animal in front of him his whole
existence through until they both decide an end of it,
and even then he does not recognize his life and this
thing coming at him with its measured tread
to be at last the same, made of one blood, one bone.

Authorized Portrait

for Eddie & Elaine Dayan

Dying to everything that needs to be done
[the falsehood of requirement]
                    so that he may live.
The face of one who is thinking death through
with a knowledge greater than knowledge,
greater than what anyone has ever known as "wisdom."
No longer a face now, but, through art,
an object in a desert landscape.
If this is to be used in a public setting:
"they" will expect immense conclusions in philosophy
                    and never find them.
Done with now. This done with. That. [How all is
done with.] And nothing left to do.
Like the miracle originally prayed for
so far back the effort to remember
                    is almost murder
[oh gardenward one dawnlight:]
                    an object totally
novel, unseen before, unheard, unthought of—
not even capable of being thought of—
the poem stands unasked for, unrequested,
without a destination you can specify.
Last needle fell he knows not when,
all needles fallen from the trees, all trees
now skeletons. And nevermore shall there be other trees:
[the very thought of "tree" unthinkable].
Acquaintances have fallen from the trees

life far too complex, too unraveling—
no bones on ground among the needles.
No birds in air, not that last consolation,
that last of freedom's definitions—the bird
rowing air's waters, his primal visage of the sea—
                    no feathers on the ground.
How deep and startled the ending verdict:
nothing to be awaited, all systems dormant,
nothing to be imagined, nothing expected,
no vision left over the screen.
And, in this silence, in this desolation,
the comfort of this ravishment,
a fresh ability to sleep,

            the quiet solace of a final beauty.

Either You Are Receiving Things Which

for Antjie Krog

no one has ever sent, or you are sending off things
which no one has ever received—and for that matter
ever will, and when I begin, when I begin to say this,
you believe I am talking [non/sense,] but it is not true,
I am talking the only sense there is which is what we do,
you and I do—and call it, what do we call it, do you know
[what we call it], when we translate a situation into life?

When the tears begin, that is the moment when
everything flows, drama is launched, when language
takes over a field which may or may not belong to it—
no one is certain, but the dark drapes are brought out,
[the dark drapes are draped over the windows anyway],
lefties walk into the room handing out messages,
interpretations concerning the great abandonment,
at which time drapes turn red and we deal not with ink

but with blood. We wish to send analyses concerning this
but no one will ever have learned the code. And we wish
to receive encouragement and comfort in the light of it
but no one will ever have memorized the words. Then what
we do, [what we do,] you and I, not to earn a living, never, no,
but simply to *tell* so that we do not die, hands us the hands
of no one; the blessing of the never-met, the never-heard of,
asking of us that we bow down and pray, that we weep, that
we conciliate the powers that be and that do not be. But it is

impossible, given the hue of human nature, and we do *not*
pray. Return to seven—sacred number, pass go, do not collect.
We suppose a stage is reached when nothing is heard any
longer, when not one word can pierce the iron-coated heart.
What do they call it: charity-fatigue? compassion-fatigue?
[which also sashays up and down with the stock market.]
Who has taken to him/herself the pain of a whole universe,

no one withheld, crushed by that whole, certainly not by "sin,"

that way then—nothing laid in the tomb, not even an absence.

The Abandonment

for Nadine Gordimer

An accusation had been leveled. No, not a single
one but many. Correct that: a multitude. Of accu-
sations. Against. This is where difficulty starts.
Whom. It seems now much too difficult to know.
[Or what the accusation had been made against.]
It has been whispered that it was against
a "what:" but one so powerful and so almighty
that daring to bring it out into the open is impos-
sible. At the Peace festival, those doves arrayed,
each on its little seat, better say throne, all spoke

out with one voice instead of singing: never
had that been known before. It was interpreted
as signifying end—that the sun, that male star,
had finally grown weary of heating earth
and puffed himself into a giant before his due
to roast earth out, to put conclusion to it.
Which then would be the only punishment
fit for an entity so powerful, so godalmighty, that
only this armaggedon could bring it down and
all, all else beside—[even if all, all else beside,]

had to come down as well. This was the sign of
the immense abandonment that left men's hearts
blasted, then petrified, and not a muscle could be
fired up again to source the hidden blood into
their organs. *Time.* This failure of the sun to happen

early now—and so to go against the grain this way
gathered no votes, no credibility. That which
had been predicted so many years back there: none
had dissected it with credence, the old prediction.
Its shortening now, even by a great span, the same.

So all lived on, as they had lived, [as if in fact immortal,
as well as deathless in the principle.] Things could get
worse a long time yet; the earth could wilt and all
things growing from it; all waters could flow back into
the sea; fearful miasmas could enfold creation:
on land, wave, cloud, no matter: the doves spoke on,
the innocent, the bountiful. "Look we have given you,
[we've given up to you,] every inherent traitor, each
plausible blasphemer—you may live safely now, laugh
ever after." What no one saw, what no one realized

in all their dreams of future happiness, which these fine
birds outlined to them in detail, was that there was one thing
wrong in the vast future schemes they contemplated,
a single thing which was not hearing them, [obeying them.]
Time, [Time indeed,] stood to them still, grown comprehensible
by this substantial cut; men's stock of answers dwindled,
because of *Time*—the running out of options, [the very
definition of an option] in the darkening air before
all eyes would sink together in the final blindness
and history as such, [as written such,] would then fade out,

cease from the persecution of the human, perish, desist.

Three Globo-Gardening Poems

1. One among Rose Gardens

Despite determinations of the landscape, soil's
poverty, absence of shade, harassments of the
blinding sun, I have persisted here toward my
pride's fulfillment in a rose garden. This grace
sits on the land—jewels at neck, wrists, ankles
of a tan princess. Piñons and junipers, oaks, hill
mahogany: green of a robe, the only one she'll
fancy, throughout history. History here is almost,
as it were, eternity (though we *know* not), under
our single time to do and love. After more work
this year than any previous, rewards have been
beneficent. Blooms have erupted suddenly and
almost all together. They have their seasons, as
the local plants, dependent on shared weathers,
a unity of all variables. The major difference
though: roses, maidenly-like, bud mornings; by
evening, they have blown out of all proportions.
After very few days, not more than a lean week,
the desert tan prevails again. I have had *one* rare
chance at a glass of buds on desk—no more than
four, where joy surprised in prehistoric days was
weeks of vases. It's what I love, what I have al-
ways done, what has sustained my life, sustains
love still. Flower's perfections, more than the
bird's (which moves, whistles, can often speak),
is *hope*—in its most elementary statement ever.

Far back recalled, it is the "pitty flower" I insisted on
in any visit, small humanoid, inspecting gardens like
an emperor's gardener in whatever lieu we traveled.
Reminds me: other dilemmas, decorations, laborsome
situations: time's throaty laughter, tragedy's ransoms.
Outside dead wars grind on into the barren sunsets, all
wars now frying heaven's roses in globalizing deserts.

2. Hummingbird-Sandwich

Bad year for hummers!—everyone says so. They
do not come to feeders. Experts say "Oh breeding
season, or weather weird" or otherwise. Bummed,
ill-humored, command the dwarfs to visit garden.
Black-chinned hummer finally accesses feeders
and I address him, in the very eyes, "Tell yr. *ami-
gos* you either come here trooping or I shall find
you in the bush and make hummingbird-sandwich.
Peace in the land! I am not truly cannibal! I swear
this is the sole antagonistic feeling felt today. The
art of gardening (I am in full discovery) is done by
instinct, not armchair knowledge, the constant ob-
servation, over as much as years, of the behaviors
of different plants, patience as great as Jove's for
any does not make it in a given year—with joy at
causing it to prosper some year after this. The art
is one as pleasing as any can be named and also is
a *healing* art—the concentration and the sweating
being such—it is impossible to dwell on great but
altogether meaner matters. And healing, not alone
to doctor here as to the patients—so some good's
done, (if not to wounded and disheartened people,
homeless and countryless, jobless and foodless, as
are the vasty millions we are supposed to feed by
frequent answers to frequent begging in the mail)
but to the songless and yet sentient plants smiling
at us with blossom or with leaf. Ergo, since these
good deeds always require one or more witnesses,
I summon ye the hummers from the immensities

lying out there in alpine desert, alpine rock. Dammit! gods, at the poet's call, no longer can descend,
finding themselves to be deficient in the clothing
of existence. So Nature must provide her testimony
to my fresh-minted kindnesses and re-wired joys.
Let hummers come in then or perish in a sandwich.

3. THE POSTETERNAL RABBIT

The sages of aforetime, muttering: "the canniest
among us: those who said *they didn't know*." Now
we say this a dozen times a morning—but it's not
wise, no—merely ignorance of how the thousand
things (make it ten thousand *a la Cinese*) can ever
possibly turn out. When will the war end? How?
Nation end? But how? The planet end? But how?
When will the leaders die, throttled for their sins,
the angles of their mouths slit to the grimace-grin
denotes the groveling apologies they never issued
while still alive? Thinkings interrupted—the dog,
must exit: sniff, shit, vision, atmosphere. Old now,
sniffs round a rhizome, freezing, staring out, for-
getful—but does not spot a thing so infinitely
minuscule I cannot figure how to link it to my
*ignoramus*ness. I see it as a baby rabbit, minute,
so *very* baby, it's hardly had the time to sniff one
sniff of this dear world. So: what's the valuation
of one baby rabbit? Compared, for instance, to a
single preemie caesared out of a mother's womb,
the mother just now shot? Is there up there among
the clouds one entity personalized who counts the
rabbits born each second on these rabbit-bearing
planets (for we are not alone), prepares for each a
golden coronet, a pair of wings in the best rabbit
fur (dyed white), a minute harp delightfully melo-
dious? So that they sing, the rabbits in the divine
upstairs that never could sing anything below. And,

interspersed with them, the singing prematures? I feel a dozen times a day *I do not know*. The world has now become so complex, there is no answer— no answering at all: — "You know, I do not know."

Mathis at Issenheim

for J.R., there

Nel Mezzo,
as man always is,
into the hospital,
for a cure to the Holy Fire,
the erysipelas, or epilepsy, or
syphilis or plague—
approaching, bloated with
sores and pus,
to find a god—

sees a divinity not just as badly off
but gone beyond that, so far beyond
that it cannot be
trounced by any other
in the lists of gods—
the suffering for once
counting beyond
the suffering of any other creature
in any where, in any when
of the whole universe,
instead of the pale, sentimental,
rather effeminate homunculus
exhibited most often whose sacrifice
cannot be *serious*,
cannot take on, so visibly, all by itself
integrally the whole pain of the world
so that you get to think
but what about? and what about?

(any initial from the alphabet,
naming the names you know):
he, she—they suffered *just* as much
sacrificed just as much, with, frequently
much fiercer pain even than just four nails
can bring to hands and feet
(the clawing hands as if imploring too)
and to terrific weight upon the upper
torso the arms, spread out, can't hold
away from heart and lungs.

Open the altarpiece to position two.
Shedding the light of morning
together with the evening's,
a magical admixture of all light,
the mother seems much larger than all others
in the presenting act of the nativity.
She bends over the present god-to-be
a beauty—no other formed of human flesh
can be compared to it. It is so pure
it has been called the "snow" and she
the Lady of the Snows—in apposition
to the great Martin's "Lady of the Roses."
The town holds these two images
of one who birthed a sun god
way back beyond what anyone recalls
of a long genealogy of births
allegedly saving men's light...

      and there is music all around
from instruments wielded by winged
beings, some in man's image, some

in the furnace of imagination still, (one
feathered, jeweled, peacock-crowned,
tinted decaying green, uncomprehending star),
as our own William Blake
might have been witness to them,
while resting in his garden.
The light falling from foreground:
young woman crowned and mitered
by fantasies to come,
will grow in time into a halo
circumferencing knowledge
both human and, if it be divined,
if it *can* be defined, "divine"
within the bounds of the imagination only.
Never forget that all disjunction's
only absolved by argument of dream.

But she, in the annunciation
looks much more like the riven lover
of our sun god (when nailed
as human in the torture scene) than like
she as a mother looks in the great presentation.
Turning of head away
from the huge messenger
imperially pointing in amethystine robes:
"you shall have this, like it or not,
and mouth no 'humble servant of the lord'
so please you—but declare right now
'I moon *shall* bear this sun of justice.'"

A mountain melts behind
the Lady of the Snows

an avalanche of light,
water returning to the summit,
the *deus absconditus* whom one must hold
defined as "father"
in his celestial rose,
small through requirements of perspective,
unutterably far
from any human pain
as he is always. Never descending.
And daughter pre-existent
clothed with the sun
in the father's mind—
with the mother human now:
daughter no longer blind
can function as the revelation
of general assemblies:
a fall undoubtedly!

No consolation
from the presented victim
of the torture scene,
awaiting you as you approach.
No sugar daddy figure
rains blessings down from sky
crooning "it's all o.k.—
you'll be here in a minute."
And no companions, not even thieves.
The sky stark black
and will remain so
and light will never seem to see again
out of dead eyes,
words never fall again

from purple maw.
No suggestion of life
behind those sockets—
this is all death, absolute death,
the nothingness itself of "nothing"
which we in thinking death cannot
encompass, absolute shutdown
of all conductors, all electricity.
The feet gone animal,
scales and smoked armor,
or like advancing roots
ready to enter ground.
The torture instrument,
hacked out from trees
is bricolaged and rudimentary:
no elegance or balance in *this* cross.
A victim has become a tree,
he is the tree that the cross hangs on,
decaying green as his opponent seems,
himself the thorns grown in and out of tree
and out the slime of all disintegration.

But, simultaneously, above a tomb
seemingly guarded by men asleep
(one man: slow-motion soldiering
his sword will not hold up
buries his nose to ground
as he pitches forward) a rose of light
features the totalizing colors of a rainbow
inside of which a figure floating up,
trailing a gown favors earth's shades
gradually melting into sky's hues,

rises from tomb, ascends, transfigures body
in a giant leap of balletic hope.
Now arms apart ready to embrace all,
face painted bright in tones of ecstasy—
only full face in all the artist's work—
as in an image which never fades,
since sun will sometimes fail our springtime fields.

The generous compulsion of these scenes!
Colossal cataract of faith,
Atlantis buried under oceans
(for it's so huge it will take oceans),
intelligence's towers drowned to the highest floor:
blind eyes of faith indeed over the waters,
floating forever on quarter truths and lies
incapable of deconstructing myth
versus the power of reality—our combat
for survival. Whose name was "Green Forest"
who made man tree—not even tree
but bark of it. A skin hardly a skin now
but just a hideous envelope to hold all pain,
insuring it would not all gush into the world
beyond the blood streaming from nails
like somber oval pupils in both hands and feet
and lance obliquely in the side. *Nel mezzo*
here again: a tale in which I could have once
believed—in this *one* canvas only.

Nothing compels belief right now in this frail tale
on which too many columns have been raised:
because if the first mother had not grabbed the apple
—*what* certified "first mother?" *what* "apple?" poison?

no son would ever have had need to die
—and have you ever known a son *not* die?
and there was no inherence in that rotted apple,
no inner cause in any "sin," no cause at all
beyond the true sores on our dying bodies,
the famines, plagues and droughts of dying earth.
Though down below men never cease from gossip,
no longer sings in sky a sun of justice now
but falls a darkness which all may take as light.

And Mathis, who accomplished this,
is still unknown in person—was only named
"Grünewald" a fullish hundred years after his death.
No will, papers, instructions, found,
virtually nothing with which to pin him down.
Might have been one of three, four, other suspects,
is said to have done this, done that,
exhibited his talent, worked in other professions,
and to have been full sadly married
yet unencumbered by ties of rank or power.
This altarpiece alone, saved over years
from many wars and revolutions,
hidden, carried away and changing domiciles
time after time for seven centuries,
saved from perdition but not so much discussed,
catalogued only among earth's treasures,
has lifted him little by little,
men's eyes sharpened for vision,
to the highest tree,
to the top branches of the highest tree,
(as lords of patience triumph over loss),
there where the stars are singing, uneclipseable.

Note

The altarpiece by Matthias Grünewald (Green Forest) (c.1475-1528) was painted c.1526 for the Antonite order of Hospital Brothers at Issenheim (or Isenheim) in Alsace, France. Hardly any art in the Western tradition surpasses it in power. It is now at the Unterlinden Museum in Colmar, Alsace.

Composed of several scenes, it was originally viewed in first, or closed, position as a Crucifixion, the most cruel and devastating ever painted, flanked by St. Sebastian and St. Anthony. The second or middle position showed, center right, a Nativity or Presentation, flanked by an Annunciation, and, center left, an Angelic Concert, flanked by a Resurrection. A third, or shrine, position featured sculptures: St. Anthony, flanked by St. Augustine and St. Jerome. These in turn were flanked by paintings of the meeting in the desert of St. Anthony with St. Paul of Thebes and the Temptation of Anthony.

The parts are presented differently at the Unterlinden.

The Concert of Angels scene contains a greenish, feathered figure thought by most to be Lucifer. Virtually alone of those present, he is not looking at the Nativity. In front, there is also a young woman, radiantly crowned and haloed, considered to be Maria Aeterna or Ecclesia.

Grünewald's life is still largely unknown. His surname seems to have changed to Grünewald a hundred years after his death—perhaps taken from someplace near a mine he worked in.

The other master painting at Colmar is the Virgin at the Rose Bush *(1473) by Martin Schongauer, and is now in the Dominican church.*

DYING TREES

ANDANTE MAESTOSO

1. The Trill

There above, there is a skylight, and a trill:
one of the household birds over my head—that
little colony of customers we have
among the richer troves of neighbor folk
with ponds and fancy feeders.
Across the view, a line of hills, a line of clouds:
they twine, a marriage of sorts, an in-out
mechanism—as marriage is, as love. Dark day
of blessing. There's plenty rain. There has not been
rain for a thousand years it seems to us, nose
dry, throat dry, smoke in the eyes for weeks.
Never they say, never it breathes but pours.
When the fires burned a month ago:
from the three States: north,
west of us, our own across the ridge—smoke
lifting haze, apocalyptic light, smothered
the morning. There is a sign among the trees,
as if some wore a robe of mourning,
the robe a desiccated brown,
a prophecy: the dead among the live, those
who'll await the once and future discontent,
those who will sleep without awakening.
Out with the dog and it's as if a world,
a world was ending, as if the bomb, [the bomb
you may remember,] had dropped at last. And not
a flower in the garden all this year, no single
flower to humor the dry heart. But, there above,
the trill. To understand! to understand something
at last: how anything is given. How anything

evolves, and where it gets to, to what end—
where all seems endless [endless in purpose,
teleology.] Will the bird's trill be a trill only?
Only a trill and past forever? In the red future?
In the abyssal present? Here plunging down to
some concretion, some fabric below which
it is not possible to go—and there it stands, the
trill, [stands?], no: suspended rather, suspended
in the restless, resting, eternity of air. And so
above, the trill. If it's not possible for me, life,
joy, in its most ancient, laughing habit—at least
the beak. Let the bird joy, live, signify there is
some purpose in the purposeless.
There is no movement forward. Despairingly,
you try to move but cannot. Yet everything
connects. Sometimes, you know, the poem can-
not stop: from day to day, a gift in fragments.

2. A Hand

In a small place, middle of somewhere
you would call nowhere, with the name,
in local language, signifying "exit,"
life, as they'd known it, ended. Death, as they'd
come to know it soon, began. The sense "beginning"
would seem to signify some life—but here
it could not. Looking across the view, wide
as a person walking many days would
take to get from left to right of it, or right to
left, a high proportion of the trees in their
fell year of drought were brown. Among the
trees still green and laughing in the sun, a
zillion beetles carried death into the bark,
branding them kin to men from then. A sound
of biting could be heard all round the area.
And here, in the mad wood, the wood become
insane through loss of green, its happy sap,
here all began again. Here in the *de profundis*.
The trees recalled a sad republic: sapped by
the same indifference, the blight of idiocy
being a death inside the men who ran her
and would carry their war into all other
empires—like beetles draculating in the trees.
Prophecy runs: absolute madness for every
single human [from the technology] in, say,
another fifty years. Pressure from the technology—
like teeth on every neck, the jugular.
What to keep in, what to keep out, that problem.
But here it all begins nevertheless.

The country has been built
over and over—so many times, and by
so many hopeful poets, in whatever medium,
claiming it never had been born, had never
run the race, had rotted in the process of
enriching shit: it having yet to be invented,
elaborated, raised from zero ground into
the empyrean. Skyscrapers had not done it,
not raised it truly over all the land
around, the huge, thirsty expanses dry as
the dustbowl of our present time, choking
the trees. Now there's to be some talk of hands—
one hand especially that has grown old, spotted
and veined in honest work and honest "husbandry."
But that is not the word: the hand is female—so
why not wifebandry? There lying, resting in the
heart of cloth, [flatters the warp and weft of cloth,]
lying much like a hand that has no work to do,
on this a poem day, a crucial one—except to signify
it will come back again to work as follows.
Out of that "exit" lived so long ago,
a lifetime seeming now, though but a year
or two, the hand draws love to it, respect
and honor, a tenderness only can be expected
for that which burgeons. So, continuity is the
solution to the problem, as it has always been,
while melancholy never lifts, but sails like
clouds, veiling the mind, a seeming permanence.
So: cloud. Cloud cover shifts, the only model, the
swiftness of the change, [how definite, how endless
is the change] a definite indefinite—clouds scud
across the sky, never to shine again. We too,

that hand and I, this hand writing this down.
I'd say this dawn, for poems never reach an
evening now, a night where they may bed them
down, looking for all the world as they were
meant to look in a once living mind. But look in
dying hand and heart, sole organs of our procreation
here, gates to a stanched desire, a curtained
universe, tenderness-covered—though howsoever maimed.

3. A Smile

A drought, from the declining of the planet,
[clogged from polluted and depleted breath,]
falling behind the shadow of a failing sun,
a sun flaring in a great rage against this end,
weakens the place's trees. Ghost beetles,
smelling the dying from two miles away,
rush to the place, a Halloween gone mad,
devour their way, quite audibly, from tree
to tree. The landscape's mouth, great smile
full of live teeth, ages in a few days—the teeth
turn brown. Within a few more weeks, trees
will shed needles, then remain black,
specter-shaped growths on the land's health. How
many years we give mankind from all this folly
to come to bare survival, then fall… then
disappearance from the scene complete… so that
the earth alone survives and remains safe? All now
seems fighting: for time and little else—against
cosmic collapse. The mother Juniper,
waves with her many yellow hands,
her hands tipped off by moths, endless
farewell to father Piñon, as if ghosts burned.
Do you remember monks burning among the trees
that many years ago? No, you've forgotten them
and so much else? Seven cool million tons of bombs;
thousands of prisoners tortured, burned, maimed;
five hundred guiltless murdered in a ditch
[among the pain recorded—how much not?]
defoliation, that especially, the dying trees around

the dying monks? Within this scheme [for nothing
leaks from "everything exists in the beginning,"]
a devastated head, beauty devoured by age, needles
of grief worn deep into the skin, small rivulets
of patience also, running down cheeks
into the chin and neck: the mirror image of the face
that's watching it across the room, a face
broken on the same wheel, a marriage wheel
of fortune—though all's been positive to date!
Even the grief! Time passes and will not
be seized in any way, will not allow itself
to be held down by its frail shoulders,
arrested, stopped there in its tracks, to be enjoyed.
It must, alike all else, be seized against the wind,
caught on the wind—"eternity" some said. Yet, still
from time to time, the smile may flash, the smile
still dazzles and whole lives light up—as if
illuminated by a tender fire, a burning, not
destructive of our wood, but granting life, quick,
urgent life, inclusive patience and refreshing love.

4. Sadness, They Say My Home

Sadness, they say my home, sadness,
what is the sadness say my life my living,
a diagram of death inside transparent flesh,
bonework jutting out right and left from spine,
building that prison-house from which no one emerges;
sadness, pool swum in one whole life, without an exit,
without a single daydream's exit any time,
moment, of day, of night, sadness: the motionless,
the inescapable, the color drained of color, tint drained
of tint, brightness of brightness, drained of all light;
sadness, the breath of flowers, the breath of birds,
the breath of simple things weaning from desolation,
the working permit of a dried up bone, the ghost
of all things tainted and disturbed. Now tired, now
desperately weary, the broken step and stagger,
the failure of the day, of every single day, of every
effort climbed along the ridges of a giant mountain,
climbed once again and one more once again and n;
sadness, the burden of our nights, blind nights and sleepless,
more sleepless than you there could ever think of being
sleepless, bone stuck into your ribs, holding you up,
something you think might be the spine;
sadness, I do not know, I do not carry knowledge,
I have no pocket for the secret prayers, I cannot think,
I cannot think philosophy, I cannot tell you life, or tell you
death, sadness because, sadness-preoccupation,
sadness the ancients used to call the "melancholia,"
blackness, the dying of the trees over the massive landscape
that caused this sorrow now, broke out an artery, opened

the veins onto the ground, letting blood flower—
but colorless, neutral and gray at times, anemic after sex,
rampant like lust at others, hot blood spurting out crimson;
sadness you see my house, never to heal, everyday house,
every night house, never to be departed from, never again
to be beginning but always end, sadness an ending
of all things, the breaking of all things, the life I cannot leave—
the dark sun of this weeping, molten moon,
what is that star of sadness in the sky, behind the sun,
that cannot ever set, and cannot ever break, and cannot
ever drown into the sky: please allow dying now,
that dark abandonment among the sucked-out trees,
please allow coming home to sadness never drowning.

5. Year's End *Chamisas*

On this extensive land, end of the year is yellow.
There is no other color on the sand—just yellow and
the yellow flowers come up in species, one by one,
one post another. They heave the ground up
with their shoulders, ground breaking, lips chapping,
around the plant. Hugging the ground are the first
yellows. Taller, species by species, until the last,
leggy, so tall *Chamisa*, the one that brings
the wretched allergies. The population sneezes,
coughs, cries, sniffles and chokes, growling like
animals: even the animals twitch with their noses.
Among drought-stricken trees this year,
the yellow grows—they say the yellow of my heart,
the yellow on my breast. Down further south they call
yellows the flowers of the dead. It will make sense
even to the gold star, the star of Europe. This year
friends die away without an explanation, they go,
[I say "they've gone to Madagascar"] and do not return.
Why Madagascar I'm not sure: it seems so far away:
enough to be a place from which no one returns. There
is no explanation for this disappearance, beyond the
busyness of all, the ever-growing, all-devouring,
the comedy of time evaporating underhand, the people
looking right and left to see where it has gone. This leaves
me speechless—dropped back to silence to find the speech.
Yellows *early* this year of stricken trees. Must mean a
most important dying, a death for which there is no name—
even within the roads leading to age, it has no name—
the scientists have warned us plenty, [we know the name,]

though we don't want, can't bear, to hear it saying:
the last of worlds perhaps is what this one may mean. Going,
they said, going into the darkness with minimal complaint
is what the yellows say, keeping the color flying now awhile
where all is colorless below. Then, in the silence, the last
search for a meaning. The only place in which I talks to I,
and can expect response. On what exactly, I do not know—
except perhaps the single name of "yellow." A baptism
from the silence, a single word standing for all the words
will follow after in metonymic strings. *Chamisa*, on its
astronomic legs, [the legs of beautiful young girls maybe
from Texas], waves in the morning wind, confirming
allergies, sneezes preceding death, the dictionary of
anguish—preceding all that ever can be said before the finals.

6. The Pain from Conversation

The pain, the pain resulting from a conversation,
is unimaginable to listeners, to interlocutors,
while he or she spells out his or her meaning
oblivious to what it may speak to the subject.
The subject tries to look into the other—as if the
other were a mirror and without devolution, answered
no argument, put forth no propositions—nothing that
could be argued with, felt good or bad about, in short,
so suffered from, so terribly. As much as wanting to despair
right then and afterward, right then, to finish with it,
[never to have to think of it again]—while that's impossible
and he/she knew it. What is requested, the absolute
tautology, which has no aspirations, not one desire, not
one surge of the flesh, or of the mind, [toward desire,] for keeps
you blissful idiot: how will you ever know what an abyss
you opened up under those feet—the subject's feet, of course,
we now refer to. In night, the blinding light of night,
the blinding day of moontime, things will have edges
whether you like it or do not. They will be marked forever,
they will be indestructible in mind, they'll be remembered
age after age in this one life. Because, once and for all, after a while,
[is it not true, thinking of any definite event, that life seems long?
Terribly long?] How is it possible to be in pain so—just from a hearing,
just from a listening to some quotidian passel of dead news, but
news that passes over you like a cold wind, the wind to billow in
your shroud so soon when you're laid down? It seems worthwhile
to think of never talking anymore, of being silent as the grave
to which you are committed anyhow—just to escape that give and
take, that conversational despair. Walking down your steep hill,

on what you sometimes please to call your property,
with every tree fading from sheer devouring, the roar of chewing
inside the trunk, the cannibal and terminal exactitude of this
desperate meal—how not apologize, how not transfer that
misery from tree to self, how not repeat "I'm sorry, I'm so sorry"
time and again, touching the tree, the branch, pathetic needles
browned out like drying excrement, and soon to fall, to
carpet the dry ground, to lay waste *domus* and the hope of heaven:
how think ever again to talk, converse with anything?

7. FRATRICIDAL ROOTS

The root is failing in its pain—not the upper
root, the bronchial, but the lower root, the penile,
that which secures the lineage. In pain, the action
acted out. The "they say" about "they say" and how
money is needed now to fight the cancer. "They will be
punched into the sea, drowned, utterly destroyed,
covered by waves, becoming archaeology for later
archeologists [maritime type.]" Then there's the other "say":
how "these are being rammed inland, hemmed in, caged,
charred in their houses—not the cool sea—but terminal
annihilation of the land-trapped, waterless,
the city-less, the country-less, the land-less, minus *patria*."
It is obscene. The fratricidal strife of two related clans
which overlap, which can't be torn apart, and all their
contents; the strife unending, un-negotiable—
geography will never swallow this, it must *desist*.
How can you buy the myth of the small country—sad, packed
with ghosts from gas, torture, rape, hanging, shooting—
now said to face thrusting into the ocean:
no! even though they all took place indeed those savageries!
no: it is strong now, is powerful, ferocious, far more so than
everything arrayed against it. I come down through
the trees—if they were olive trees, if sandalwood, if
cedar, in the burning light of the low desert—where
this is high, where this can snow, where this can also
rain, bleed blood. Death of these trees stains off onto the death
of all things else. Yes, even humans. Do not ask
money, wretches, you who are always asking
money—for such and such a pain, or insult, or the

vandalism. Sickness at hearing of it, at never hearing
end of it, [and never reaching end of it,] at having
heard it since one was gotten born, in womb as
well, before the soul-formation it would seem,
in the ancestral lineage, climbing back up the tree, right
up into the origin of light. Same sadness, selfsame
wound, for beauty of it, for bomb in flower, for the strap
of martyrdom around the waist. May all the books
that talk of such self-immolate. Explode. Evaporate. May
the atrocious trinity of books destroy itself. May never be
another deity like to these deities. May exhortations,
these endless exhortations cease. May body lie
in pure, in unadulterated pain. The suffering be pure,
unwashed, unsung, yes, uncreated. May all
the cities cataract into the desert. That there be end
unto this stench. Yes that the sun burn down into
these mountains and these plains, collapse across the land.

8. Unravelling / Shock

A hole torn in the fabric of the world,
the web, the whole infernal weave
through which life-giving rain is falling
but mixing with the tears and with the blood.
Dead body-snatchers enter, the mega-corpses,
much in the news these days, enter and grind
bones, flesh and sinews down to dry tree bark,
mixing with tree bark, crawling with the demonic
beetles. They'll tell it later: "No one expected this":
not one—patient, doctors, practitioners
of every stripe, no one except the one whose daily
work is close to prophecy, who feels it in his nerves
or in her muscles—where news travels up fast
and lodges in the eyes, all-seeing, all-pervading vision
of disaster. And comes in like a mouse, wee small,
[wee modest, so wee, wee practical,] mouse with big ears
and popping eyes, looking this way and that and not
one tittle-tattle fazed by your huge presence. Later
drowns in a bucket with a lizard: everything drowns
round here getting to water. Not able to get out again.
Thus coming quietly, thus probing, [thus stealing in,]
squatting thus quietly back of the house:
how do the tears well up, well down again,
what makes them well, the seeing eyes know not,
what routes the change parent-to-orphan? Stop.
Orphan-to-parent? Stop. Then back again to tears?
Look out beyond the healthy trees preserved
in a close circle round the house for privacy,
look out the window over hills and dales

of this *milagro* country, see living green, see dying
brown—on each and every morning mourn the trees.
Criminal imbeciles who run the shows we live in
from top to bottom of their slimy theater, have now
decreed they will not solve the water. Matter of fact,
they will not solve what we are made of—the high
percentage water in all of us compounded. They will not
solve a single problem by the name of life we give
to human business. They will prefer
to dip their steel in blood, to let the semen drip
from off their steel into the blood and thus contaminate,
infuse with every cancer both body politic and body
not so politic, just private, single, individual—but
gives to other individuals their mien and color. Ghosts
walk the hills and dales between the dying trees.
"Remember now," they say, with stab at tragic countenance,
[for when can privacy enter into collective?] "those days,
those days you took no notice of, counting them poor,
dispersing them among the memories you could not value
at their true worth, you could not recognize enough to feel:
who knows if these few days, [these very days,] were not
those ones we lived together here, the only paradise?"

9. GOLDEN GLOBES OF HOPEFULNESS

Operation successful. Sentinel node unreached
by the disease on its rampaging conquest—
although pathology to follow for certification.
The golden globes, those fertile golden
globes of every size, shape, texture
available to size, shape, texture in global paradigm—
to which men's frail attention forever wanders—
but they are dangerous. They are the script
of tragedy. Small globes thrive in the larger ones,
containing each the crab, my legendary totem,
the which, in this disastrous, never-resting guilt,
I've used to kill more than the populations of the earth.
Mainly the dream-folk, broken, tongueless.
This is the last hurrah of the indigenous:
the time we take the land from them—for come what may,
whether we're left or right in politics,
we need the land and suffocate to seize it.
Land, gas: a time of spoils approaches. Criminal oilmen
and their puppet maniac can only daily croak Irak Irak.
There are good reasons for terminating this
Irak Irak. My father never shot his wad Irak Irak.
And now, the rain this morning. Brown trees,
the dying in their thousands—that were not born for death
immortal trees—continue drying. But rain shows up the green
push of the young, at tip of each live branch, standing in contrast,
[sometimes in brilliant contrast,] right up against a brown,

and hope, kin to the overwhelmed relief in re the globes,
throws a man down to floor again, again, again—into the sleep
of justice. But this, this brown, is unsustainable:
they are too few to hold the goods; *we* are too many now
not to win goods: the center cannot hold, nor the periphery—
the iron globe that feeds this rotting world
must, dry and milkless, at the morning moon bay one more time
like the coyotes of our native land. The polity
has been an enterprise so criminal from its conception
it is a miracle a tree has ever grown there, single tree
oh never mind a forest. It is at war with the whole universe
wearing its garb of peace and its angelic wings,
mouthing its dithering self-satisfaction, wafting those wings
toward Irak Irak. Once it was Nam and Nam
and then the targets getting ever smaller
until the giant strike on Glorious Grenada. But now,
it grows again, inflates, swelling the iron globe
[we shall have empire on the entire world] except the globe
is black as sable, black as ink this time,
black as burnt human skin
to the utmost degree. Hope, only source of poetry,
chickens its way out of this heaven into no other hell.

WAR STILLS

Group One

1. A Marsyas Effect

Walking among the trees, an emerald patch,
a reminiscence of long ago: was it a painting,
was it this person painting, was it another? Sun
is the basis. There is a basis here for what is ailing.
There is a shred of love among the greens, love of
locality: a local recipe for loss of voice, for suffocation.
The floor goes through a floor, goes through that floor,
goes on through every floor into inferno. The walk continues
without alternative. A dignity arises from the emerald patch,
the only dignity this walking thing can think of—reduced
to thing by adverse circumstance. Never so low: [in all
the years, never so low.] An evidence: of only this, of
only that—but such things *things*, not spirit: [sun forbid
they should be spirit.] Far off, in an infinitude, a war
progresses. It is the third or fourth similar war—the moves
are clear from the beginning, except for analysts
of military adventure and who the hell cares now for such,
for specialists? There are the ones who specialize in killing
and those who specialize in dying; the hospital
is full on the first day, the doctors few and, after all,
folk have been dying now for some considerable time
due to a strangling process the killers have perfected.
Sun is on the side of killers, not of the disappearing. And then
the four or five distinguished leaders of the killer pack
blather their way through t.v. show [and t.v. show again:]
the awesome scroll of t.v. shows, the never ending

mis & dis: [disinformation raw.] Walking among
the local trees, an overpowering desire to witness
Marsyas. Hanging from his own tree, he's upside down,
his testicles tightened with string, good and strong tightened
like a dictator and his mate back in nine four o five
among the trees of Italy, those lovely columns. Multiply
Marsyas by four or five and you complete the picture
of a familiar situation under our guilty noses.
They've failed abysmally to justify the language.
This is to speak of war, [for all now speak of war]
and it is seemly to show some opposition. Down on the
lowest floor, where ice is made by the machines
that Marsyas had bought, weapons of mass destruction,
Titian's delight, in his late art, delineates
the flaying to perfection. A dignity, an evidence, an
effervescence even. See what one does with paint!
The emerald glow of undersea—with a strange smell,
the skin peeling away from muscle and from bone,
the stench of traitors to a cause, predators gathering.

2. The Fire Season

a]
This writing, this activity,
may supersede the fire season.
Air is heavy—but "brighter
than a thousand suns" with just
the measure of a single sun. Smoke
spreads over the mountains as if to disappear them
[and what in this foul season is never disappeared?],
drowns them in a white sea as white as Arctic.
You can imagine the animals
coughing and wheezing with their last breaths
and the live ferns curling into fetal positions.

b]
They know nothing of this in the East.
They would like to have a smidgeon of your drought.
They sit in their diminutive offices
watching the rain patter on every pane,
working on their degrees in mental cruelty.
In this the heartland of information ages
their wires sing over grave's silence.
The West has always been under an Eastern thumb—
our West has said so. Hills now breathe in
the West's frustration. This is the facet of the poem
that you are now allowed to call "confessional."

c]
Our pines continue to die and continue to die—
funeral carpets of needles around their base.
You could sleep there, you could suffocate

soundly and be in harmony with all of nature.
You no longer know what keeps you from dying,
what keeps you walking, climbing, falling
down to the gullies of a lifelong sleep,
what encouraging music keeps the heart beating:
that surge of live surf in your ears,
the hiss of fire racing through the forest
with a Trojan smile fading among its towers.

d]
We are not far removed from that city. We have
just conquered it. I am not told yet
how many trees it had, how many it has lost.
We were not told to guard its treasures from our fire,
how many centuries of treasure the fire melted down.
There are you see those livid penalties
which strip your face off from your skull,
the lining off your heart and off your muscles,
wearing your knees to bring you down to them.
And you will never swallow them,
never allow the fire to sear your guts,
no, not in a thousand [thousand lifetimes]
because the very life of life for you is justice.

3. The Asphyxiation

Needful, while it is taking place,
that the process be invisible
both to the executioner and to the victim.
For now, let's say the victim is your honor,
the judge-role done with and the robe burned.
Guerrilla war is universalized: the whole world
is the menace now, we see the enemy
at every gatepost: our law alone is
liberation. Kerchief, or gag, whatever,
to be as black as Chinese ink,
whole face as well covered in tulle,
this black of course—as in those plays
where scene-shifters don black to sign "invisible."
Interrogator, interrogators, to be most normal folk
such they could be exchanged for any other folk
and no one, [none, no one,] would ever be
so much the wiser. Sitting
most days in offices, filing bland duties
like mostly paperwork and such banality.
All this though all the prisons melted down:
the world may witness we are white as sheep.
No one in town to know the difference
one way or either. So that, to go to town, to greet
one's friends implies the occultation of the strangled
scream inside the throat that swallowed gag or kerchief
in the act of living. And you say "fine," yes, "fine thanks,"
"fine" again [and always "fine"] until the end of publication.
"How are you doing this fine morning?" "—Fine, how are you?"
the language plumbs the depths of idiocy

hoping you all and sundry will make "enjoy your day."
The eye of judgment sits the Adam's apple,
continues unrecorded in any document.
And you go home to swallow time
as if, on the first day, you'd swum the sea
to find on coral reef the skull of judgment—
with throat now free of all encumbrance
since you had mastered the asphyxiation.

Group Two

I. ON "SOUL" AS ALIBI FOR ALL HYPOCRISY

a]
They say that inner nature is revealed by your
appearance. Unlikely that. In fact impossible:
for one thing, *inside*'s thick, [extremely thick,]
whereas the *outside* is thin as can be. Looking
inside, you'll find only a butcher's shop: every
commodity in there is bathed in blood. Whereas
outside manifests healthier, more pleasant tints:
innumerable shades of cream, coffee, and black.
You could not possibly enjoy the life *inside*—
perpetual stench of blood, vomit, excrement.
Some claim the *inside* is the abode of "soul"
but what we have agreed so far would make this
"soul" a bloody property. How is it possible
to swear that your discovery of "soul" will
purify both you and the whole universe, when,
"soul" bloodies every and all the true indigenous?

b]
Now there *is* a place, [there *is* a place,] true
far off from us, but where it's possible to touch
a kind desire, though age will steal it from you
and leave you dying of remembrance. But age…
will also now have claimed the lover's looks. At
the appointed time, you can return into the inner "soul,"
should you insist on taking that direction, and
end your days in the atrocious hells you have created.

c]

Forests fall, lakes dry out, sky's hazing from its
blue profound to an unhealthy shade of gray.
The tribes die out for lack of peace and weather:
their land, their members' bodies raped out of
countenance. Neighboring peoples whose every
interest would seem reciprocating kindness, murder
each other day after day while suits dream of
Armageddon in one or other cockpit, making their
millions cheerfully from both sides' armaments.
And there's no need to add coveys of politicians.
Criminal castes of c.e.os pocket their astro-
gnomic bonuses while selling us the latest gross
utilities. Now their Armageddon is massive war.
Diplomats come and go dreaming of modernism.
But neither they nor we can see Megiddo truly.
Ours is the inability to recognize the real abyss
opening up below the householder, i.e. the death
of every inch of common ground this planet offers.

2. On *Infoglut* in the Wake of Pindar

The window on death remains the same size—yet
the window widens, embracing all information.
Teevee, the universal snack, our only venue now.
We are frozen by these sights we see as in a mirror,
[as in a mirror of our inner state] declared precisely
to those guarding all borders. We no longer *can* care
how many died today, this month, this year,
irrespective of sides in the world conflagration,
because, once beyond statistics, the body of care
freezes in its uniform of ice. We, the few fortunate.

Joyfully we poets access existence, joyfully praise the
day, joyfully praise the organs of the victors, joyfully
dispatch the losers to their graying homes, their tearful
hometowns now torn and decimated. The dark of other
seas surrounds us, *our* sea of light advances gratefully.

The hero's wife died on that plane, all on board died—
while Rome burned. If the story be told he wants *reality*;
he wants every detail to be told in detail: beating down
imagination completely. He has no need of art, the story
to be absolutely faithful to the landscape in his head.
And why did not a single person involved in that project
mention the compassionate depiction of the murderers,
how too they suffered the failure of their martyrdom,
relative to the original scenario. All things in this life
come differently. Nothing is ever on call, nothing on
time—not even our imagination of blessed poetry.

"Thelord" kills as much as it saves, perhaps more.
Prayer is unheard except by the sender of the message.
Terrible, "The Lord of Hosts" raises the "real" in the wind,
terrible as an army with weapons of mass destruction,
devastating the land and its walls even as far as Eden,
which is to say all the land there is we came to devastate.

Group Three

1. HANDS

Let these smiles, after triumph, return into their mouths.
[Into their mouths:] I want not one of them, nor smiles,
nor mouths. On the floor a closed box. Can it contain
persuasive numbers of human hands, cut from their too
possessive bodies? Is it *natural* that a body should need
its hands? Not in this present circumstance, not in these
politics. Evanescent, rapturous clouds dream way above
the mortal scene while soldiers move forth under orders,
sliding round walls, darting from post to post, kicking
doors in with their remaining feet. A dark within there,
darkness of poverty devoid of fire or even lamps, a dark
lost to pretence. Asleep. Three to kill, one to rape. Pre
the rape [three dead,] a substantial explosion, a suicide
against an outer wall. Nontrivially, the soldiers turn into
heroes—in such a time as this, the gods dream in their
towers of all mankind's awards and medals. Also okay,
the soldiers are hurt bad, break into sweats, wait rescue.
In rush the paramedics. After consensual red crosses,
minute orgasmic beings are introduced into the warrior
bodies, bent on their labors of repair. A new leg here,
arm there, the third receives pretty metallic brains will
keep him in sweet dreams his life-long through. Hands
take the girl's attention from her trials. What though
they have emerged from other nations, they amply have
the personality of lovers, the kind you find at home. She

lies back in a trance while the fine clouds descend into her
eyes & make them merry. All round discrete applauding.
A tiger then laps at the lowest fountain of her blood. The
finals of the age of simulations? All round discrete applause.

2. Soft-shell Crabs

This fight, this struggle, will you ever believe it,
part of all struggle for the world's survival? Pa-
thetic in its smallness, this soft-shell crab puts up
defenses against a humvee. Burnt to its bones,
the crab is taken off wrapped in a cloth: they will
pretend it's human. Survivors palaver with their
wrath of god, their hands put up defenses to their
lips. Speaking to you in an old secret language
you no longer, poor infants, understand. You did
not prep, [you did not read,] you are not scholars.
The sad old vehicle moves on a hundred feet, is
blasted to the roofings of the city for its pains. Ah
war on terror how much oil has run on down under
this bridge, vehiculating mouths, bones, stratagems,
while prices soar over the civilized & sassy s.u.vs.
Most generals, with names tenfold repeated on their
chests, yet medals left more modestly at home on
those spare uniforms fit for s.u.vs, declare hot sea-
son on the soft-shell crabs victims of foul indoctri-
nation. We'll kill the far-fetched scum when we have
caught them, never you mind, there's victory ahead!
Back in the palatine far mountains, small joyous fires
light up in celebration. Princes not apprehended yet.

3. La Città Morta

Iarba ochilor tăi, iarbă amară.
Flutură vânt peste ea, pleoapă de ceară.

Apa ochilor tăi, apă iertată.

Paul Celan

The city lies under the waters, [the city lying under
the sea] if it comes to that—one way or the other,
innumerable dead floating on the waters; countless
houses, & debris of houses, [floating on the waters.]
No one has sent, [no one has sent] anything for help.
Pain absolute solitude. All else, communal, dies.
Or walks out of the city never to home again. See:
Bourbon Street lies in the green zone & the bombs
with men strapped to them explode under the waters.
Men's fashions sway on by; women's [sway on by,]
lashings of cleavage plunging: the eternal opium
of cleavage. In submarine sport, nation A defeats
nation B which defeats nation C—*und so weiter*:
the fans swim up & down, howling and gnashing
teeth. Books are produced, music produced, art
is produced & all of it is duly performed. Under-
water the drowned enjoy all these productions. A
very few, sitting on house roofs above mother sea,
[enjoy all these productions.] The leadership's collec-
tive testicles will fry in oil—under the detestation
of plebs deprived of voting machines. *Ave Maria*'s
sung in all the churches as an antidote to cleavage.
The sad drowned are the only poor left in the land

since all the other poor have been sent for a soldier.
Suddenly, the nation is cleaned of its disadvantaged,
everyone is rich and thanks go up among these rich,
thanks go up to the leaders, now re-machoed in time
for future elections. They'll go back once again & go
back [once again, & go back once again, & again &
again] to the white father of cities at the inland heart—
until the sea behaves & shivers back to *its* homeland.

MOVEMENT /

NORTH OF THE JAVA

SEA

Ascending Flight, Los Angeles

"It is characterized by a pale subtle happiness of light and sunshine, a feeling of bird-like freedom, bird-like altitude, bird-like exuberance, and a third thing in which curiosity is united with a tender disdain."

Friedrich Nietzsche

1.

Seen face to face in domestic converse:
no compassion. Seen in a group of persons
in social converse, none either. Seen solo
waiting, far off and isolate, colorless as
a grounded, wingless, songless passerine,
compassion's ocean rises, flooding chest
chasm, a fraction further, extrudes tears up
and into eyes. Here, vastness of the Angels'
heart downtown, close to all arts and music,
sparsely filled up with buildings, their al-
zebras in crazy inundation of Californian
light. Always a few degrees above our own
and riotous with varied flowers and greens.
Airwise, blinding green parrots and such e-
xotica as might seem to belong here crackle.
Little Tokyo, Little Beijing, good rebates on
blouse-grown wings. The tears sink down to
rest in curiosity. Inveterate explorers wake.
Abandoned leftwing veterans rot on streets.
Beyond a world mayhem continues. Crying
sees murder; curiosity: consumption. Through-
in a day, hang out, eat, drink, shop & consume.

2.

Birds from colorless to color; flowers color
to colorless. To stop life's turn to nightmare
adopt the colorful patience of birds. Flowers
take flight and become birds, add color to
the birds in sky, so high, their colors hit in-
visible. This is the level we desire to reach:
bird high, plant low—*famose* cosmogony.
Out there in Hollywood, air-breasted women
trying to become birds and failing even, why
at ascent to flowers! To conjugate, lone mind,
all that is beautiful way and above all man, &
human understanding. Planes in their traces
along sky move white from unknown city-
unknown city, and this for no known purpose
you can witness low—but bird is clear in
purpose how much high, as hummer was at
nose the other day while gardening. Since I
was raising flowers to the power of air. As
child, remember Mitchell in the movie, eyes
up intently at a lone seagull—and she'll be
loveliest ever to fly, him whispering, and so
she was in metal clad, flying countries alive.

3.

In cities, when the noise by day is overwhelming,
birds have evolved in time to sing by night, thus
to be heard by other birds. That's what we birds
are doing now, that once were poets of the day.
We sing at night, all hope on standby, but we *are*
heard by our own kindred. Meantime, deliberate,
people may rot into sweet angeleños. We crummy-
nals! dropping them there while shopping! O! O!
Wait! Wait! For ages now I shall read selfsame,
very same book over and over, not skipping book-
book, place-place, or landscape-into-landscape.
I'll persevere presentially with one enlightened
me, ago when we could climb not even castles.
My darkness lifted and, suddenly made mirror, I
sent back simple verbs to one scale of our time.
Emotions are dead leaves; yet some may carry
to sing as if a world were morning, as if light,
still tinted by the birds, were truth and possibly.
After the night, after angelesque dreams, a great
light sphere rolling into the room, a rubber cage
with convict bird inside—clothed in all colors
the despised can dream. World granted. Novel day.

SUN'S CLOUDS

for Nathaniel Mackey

On billionth trillionth evening of the world
by one man's estimation,
gigantic cloud pivots on itself
wind-launched contrary,
dark, fearsome beast, mountain-tethered,
downing from the Sun's house,
swims up again, alive
in the full circle of its emptiness.
Wind, temperature, interminable cycle.
Sky loses contrasts,
palest blues, high cirrus filaments,
swallowed by rising animal—
all now one darkness.
What has at times been called the "soul,"
          the reception clerk,
                    infolded, shivers.

Palm tree,
towers over all vegetation,
thrashing its arms in wind,
frustrated gladiator
unable to reach prey,
changes to work below:
foul octopus all eyes
scoping all ocean,
brims up the sea with rage,
takes up whole space almost,

which is but mirror of the sky—
cups sucking, closing in
                  on whales, on ships.

An undulation music of the whale,
backwash a pounding of the tail,
north summer-bound,
searching its way into the dark,
which, powered by the Sun in its foundations,
churns ocean into light.
Stars too are guiding
birds on their northern passages,
playing with all directions at one time,
yet moving winds together
                  toward the northern ice.
Behind all these

volcano shadow
they call house of the Sun
wider than span of cloud,
of gladiator's arms,
than the far side of his left eye,
than the far side of right—
and from this mountain Sun arises,
angry out of his palaces on earth:
earth seared for centuries
without our calculating it:
the cloud masking his fire,
what seems so green at times
                  a coat of darkness.

And all desires

drunk by the giant cloud,
losing the element expectancy
in one man's estimation,
quell terror in the "soul"
   which, satiated, slumbers.

Haleakala, Maui, 03. 2001

SELF AND OTHER

Not this self the miracle
but the miracle is the self of another,
radical quantity
not tethered to this self
nor this self tethered to that other—
the utter solitude of worlds
which do not need to pass in the night
like the proverbial ships
to recognize the loss, [absolute loss]
of anyone to any other—
the loss continuing
as it were "forever," there being now
no exact exit from the solitude.
Zero tolerance in the fates
for the atrocious suffering of the partition
that a one might spend a whole existence
with another and yet the tethering
never occur—[not once in, what,
seventy / eighty years: a lifetime?]
This is the greatest "sin" among the sins
once named "original," the sin that drags
down life below itself in that
creation must wrestle with this sin,
never redeeming or redressing it,
yet in eternity knowing time's
total estrangement from all other time,
never at ease with human kind,
[nor yet unease with humankind,]
but just the fortitude,

but for the grace of,
just waiting for the drinks,
the appetizers,
in other "words,"
to reach the pool and staring at
a new arrival. Talk of significance
mere sparrow shit. Now, simultaneously,
a burning interest in the next facet
of this life and then the absolute
desire to put an end to it.

[*as from Peliatan, Bali, 07. 2004*]
[*But for the grace of*]

A Language of Absence

for Joseph Donahue

That this substance
sustained in the complex of other substances
and forwarded to linkage with
substance everywhere
should, if a balance,
if a balance were to be upset
between absence and presence
with thousands of dead
of a sudden one morning:
the impurity of that
would conceive an absence
of the *whole* system
for a considerable time.

✦ ✦ ✦

White starling virtually extinct,
emblem bird of this place,
down to two couples left in the wild,
the balances of mating,
raising in nurseries
not working out
because young birds released
fly straight into the sun—
loitering hawks
seizing those bodies of light
turn them to blood.

Something unreal in this
which is to say dream-like
but not in the movie sense of "dream."
Rather an unreality
designs our absence,
attacking all such places
known by the name of "paradise"?

✦ ✦ ✦

Turning to night.
Darkness descending
sits itself down in small,
extremely narrow seats set high for the gods
at the summit of temples,
above shimmering waters,
gorges, ravines
in their devouring splendor—
gods but children
and terror-struck.
Blood of the past, flesh of the future
this substance
[substance real or imagined:
is there a difference]?
How will it last, this substance
blessed with the name of "island,"
volcanic though secure,
folded over on itself innumerable times—
"island" which all have agreed
is "paradised" by "beauty"
since when *les immémoriaux*
primed their decrees?

Island which nothing ever reached by water,
nor from the air, which remained ever
untainted in its storm of seas,
the same birds waking everywhere
at the same time with the same song
and waking up all else.
Rise of "fair women"
fairest of creation,
none fairer ever fashioned
since the emergence
and wherever anyone looked
into the furthest corners of the world
none like them could be found.
Moving half naked to their work
and to their pleasure
mais où sont les seins d'antan?

◆ ◆ ◆

Desiring to be naked
to be the fruit of pure desire,
imperial death shivers in its clothes,
wills away clothes,
innumerable skins—
a multitude of clothes shaking
as the invisible body
ponders its shadow play.
Now enters the absence.
Flame springing tree of life,
trembles behind a screen:
now you see one side, now the other,
whole populations of beings

born of emergence,
depending from its branches
and the fire blazing,
the bodies of all the shadows
thrown on the screen—
dance thrown at evil,
evil lying down in terror
at thoughts of dying from the world.

✦ ✦ ✦

All is absent here—be sure of it,
even the light illumines nothing
and the birds are nothing flying through nothing.
It is not possible to recognize
any familiar sight
for sight, hearing and smell are absent
and the tactile orders
of both normal and abnormal substances.
Where *is* this we continue asking,
is it the hidden part of the "great way,"
[used to be called great way,]
is it the section talked about for eons
but never described,
[could not be described?]
Yet music behind the music
music guessed at by the ear,
that runs from ear to ear
like a great river:
this you can sense you hear
although no noise at all
pierces this absence.

Mother of temples
eternally removed
far as another galaxy,
yet feeding these
the daughter temples
with holy water.
It was found one day
not quite as far as reckoned
but on another island,
huge, pregnant—all earthly rivers
from its four gates,
flowing toward the daughter temples
from the maternal lode.
High on the upper platform
you sit on your smallest throne,
await a sunrise from behind a mountain,
perfectly formed volcano
while mists swirl up and down
surrounding heights
revealing substance in its dream of glory.

Arriving in the night
before that sunrise,
the verse concocted to perfection,
impossible to lose,
[not written down
no way you could forget it]—
and in the morning

totally forgotten.
It would have been
perfection of perfections,
all problems,
meanings reconciled,
"language" arising from the "dream" of stone.

Besakih, Bali - Borobudur, Java, 06. 23 - 26. 2004

The Island Weavers

That there should be islands. Specified by the
ocean which needs a place to rest its waves. In
the great deep, you understand—not neighbors
to familiar coasts. The islands should be green,
not common green but devastating green. With
green that, seen at sea, takes out the eyes of
sailors and blinds them to all colors else. Each
made up of a vastitude of trees. Edenic garden.
But pyramid from the *peripleukos* view, as if
there were a central trunk and the whole island
were single tree at heart. Tree's base: a cave
and, in the cave, a weaver. All have the divine
right to that—if not divine, then human should
suffice. As travelers swirl round, they deem
any one of these islands—the one detected and
approached—is a home once owned for eons.
For not one of these travelers totals a human:
there is some wariness as to their status. What
they have harbored dreams of for so long is that
this should be truth of any traveling—that any
island whatsoever reached, including those they
journey on to later, should feature a same tree,
that cave, that weaver. Where they arrive, and
at that place alone, a host of strangers gathers in
the entrance and pleads daily and nightly with
the weaver. By definition, though, by protocol,
she will refuse. She does not still await a homer.
She has long lost all interest in that. It's only
that she knows every lone roamer has this dream:

not that he will be known but that he's recognized.
And taken by the spirit of the place. And that the
spirit bears the place's name and is his addict for
that place. These hierogamies were structured long
ago, struck to the very texture of all things and of
the total song of thing. There's no deletion possible.
While the oncomer takes unlikely, childish pleasure
in the birds' colors on the many trees, the weavers
sing a music which he has never heard before. Yet
he suspects he is familiar with that music and with
the air foaming above the pyramid, floating the birds.
Feel free to switch the "he" into a "she." Some men
weave too from time to time among perilous waters.

Kimbe Bay, New Britain, Papua New Guinea, 08. 2006

SARAWAK

Ins and Outs of the Forest Rivers

in memoriam, S., activist

"Les rivières sont des chemins qui marchent et qui portent où l'on veut aller."   Pascal

"It is not certain that the speaker is the hero for it may be he who listens."
                              "The Heroes at Kapit, 1815," ms.

Famished for the totality,
forever, still, again,
sampling yet another part,
moving out once more
toward the expected
but unknown flag
high on a mountain top
at this extremity of the tropic world.
Car to the airport late, friend
nervous and uncommunicative,
bookstore phone line down,
credit card therefore useless,
not a nickel left in cash, bank
a.t.m. machine swallows my card,
bird-watching book not acquired.
A poor beginning.
The plane is at the gate
a thousand steps away in this
crazy airport—the gun jumped
by this country once again
into a "higher" stage of "progress."

Weather is foggy, hazy, masks
an undertow begging to be revealed.
A seabed waits for you,
has waited since time began.
History enters the present
like a river into the sea.
This may well surprise you
but today is the day that you die

In the interests of solitude
that the void might conjure up a world,
nothing to be left at your back
from which any recall could proceed,
the river to run unimpeded into any sea
it might choose to drown in, the forest
to spring upward into its canopy,
the line between earth and sky
uninterrupted, with passage to and fro:
all the high birds in their sprung freedom
eating of fruit ripened by heaven

Entrance into the forest. In trance. At start
everything slithers, first of all two feet,
inadequately shod, on slimy roots and branches,
everything drips, face drips, the right
side neck gland drips high in the nape,
the forehead into eyes, chin drips, nose, cheek,
hat itself drips—only gods know how—you stand
there watering the earth as if it were a garden.
Noise of the insects, a noise eternal
which never stops for birth or death
as bugs relay their sound through centuries.

Ditto the calls of birds—but "bird"
itself remains invisible high in the canopy,
will not come down for drowning man to glimpse.
A leaf will drop: no, it is not bird,
a movement here or there: it is a butterfly:
the butterflies in forest surrender to the eye
but the bird not: prefers to place a leaf
over its face and say "Cuckoo! Yes, I *am*
bird—but *you* will never read me!"
And finally the unexamined lives of all
these trees so much alive and yet so
silent, these also you can see with all their
parasites, exuding life with generosity
unparalleled in all the kingdoms. A single
giant especially, *dypterocarp*, couple of hundred
feet up into sky, its crown a jewel
of that ceiling in which, I'll swear to it,
all my birds are hiding. Trunk I cannot
embrace, diameter continuing so far
beyond my hands—and yet I wish I could,
more than a grandfather, so awe-inspiring
are reach and fretted bark. And then the silence
underneath the noise, refusing to allow
the planet a green death, the accidental scenes
of the two-legged animals slaving and slavering
to bite this treasure down with their steel teeth

Every time you move to the forest's edge
you meet it sooner. Forest encircles
you like a bride's corset (made up of silver
hoops among these tribes). Forest will choke
you if you move carelessly, without

extremes of circumspection. The animals look
haunted: they run into each other far too often.
Birds find overmuch to feed on in the canopy.
They fly in circles, caged by the borders
imposed by bulldozers and other noise-makers.
It is the vastness of the forest over-shrunk.
Note, one pointed out, of all these surrounding
mountains only that small part over there
about a tenth, is free of cutting—and now
they've got concessions for that tenth and
even villages sink into their maelstrom,
because of having to give up their choicest trees,
the ground infertile and unhallowed,
their fields unable now to raise the rice

A plant moving slowly overhead—part of
the wall of trees in motion—aha! a bird!
But it is not, merely some current of the air
invisible to you makes that leaf shiver.
Cut out the motor of your thin canoe,
an able tide-devourer, you are in heaven,
or in a dream with things passing intangibly
as if by wisdom hallowed. It is eternity,
it's moving in unrecorded time you may
have witnessed once in a night cyclo-ride
as ten young monks made the noise of thousands
back in Angkor, prepping their recitations
like centuries ago. And now. Never again

Sometimes it is my pleasure to become
obsessed with one of many subjects: this
time the predicate is "bird." I slither through

an unknown land with a methodical thirst
for a knowledge which will quench the desire
and cause it to desist. Leeches drain flush of
blood runs crimson down my legs and arms
while small thought-strokes from time to time
destroy what can't be bird in mind—which
is to say destroys all things that are not forest.
This purification will also satisfy the apes
astride the branches quietly in trees like
ripened fruit about to fall, the tails sometimes
hanging straight down, bell cords to pull—
unknown to them the trees themselves
they sit on will very soon be cut
for a few hours of heat or light as far away
as death is near to forest. "Up close and personal"
they call this thirst to know completion of the
catalogue before the very last of trees collapses
so that we are aware of what we've lost
we that have not achieved full-scale humanity

I do not know the sea this river ends in,
Sulu Sea it says, yes Sulu it says
on this new map—but I can check no evidence
of Sulu in this mist devouring all
phenomena. Sungai Kinabatangan,
a most melodious name you repeat day-long,
the name reverberating day-long in your head:
a narrow strip of virgin forest left untouched
on each bank of the rivers
making the small ones look like gates to Eden
in which they end by crowding animals
so tight they can be seen by tourists ignorant

of all the implications. (Besides, these look
only for monkeys, leave out all other wildlife
because that's what the guide-books say to see).
While all around, thousands of miles, stretch
olive-palm plantations: most economical and
most remunerative but dry as dust and cash.
Upriver, silt and debris from the cuttings
menace the water from its head on down. It's
said you cannot bathe or drink in rivers anymore

Trapped in pervading stench of old ideas,
trapped in repetitive paralyzed projects,
trapped by the magistrates who never move
on cases dusty for decades, and by police
who police nothing but the new owners' acres
they took from those who grew the land
and are now homeless. The forest drips
a thousand years of water from every tip
of every branch mourning its lords, much
as the rocks in the high caves drip greater spans
of time to reach aspiring stalagmites. If this
were blood, the whole land would run red.
Trapped in the monologues of ancient stories,
invisible birds and heroes sound their songs
but no one's there to hear them. My own ears
age—day by day I can hear less of birds
who sing the tribal sorrows for lack of poets.
All fades to elegy. Deadened by repetition,
I try to hear the words in birdsong, attempt,
by swallowing remnants of beauty, not to lose hope.
Colleague ends up by whistling like a bird

Speed through the forest's arteries,
(the blood of talk, of work, of war),
through Malian, to Tutoh, into Baram,
five hours from here, Batang Baram,
mother of rivers. There are no words
for this: it is another world. It is
expressed in a foreign tongue, a host of
tongues—not in your terms, your codes,
you fancy folk in your homes embalmed,
no, nothing can be parried to your query
"Have a good trip?" In fact you do not want
to know what you cannot know in those other
languages—so all is well. And the great rigs
barreling down from the raped mountains
continue breaking forest into road-locked
parcels, bring us the matter of "our" houses, the
comforts of "our" lives—so all is well

The forest's heart explodes,
its green blood foams in the arteries
returning to the sea through a thousand
mountain walls of green untouched as yet.
Cascades of flowers several stories up,
beginning in the canopy and ending
in the river, the only signature of red.
Everything in heart's world explodes
as well, only the sapphire kingfisher
pierces the cataracts of emerald blood
avoids a drenching, moves to further fish.
In a boat that tips at the breath of a
dragonfly, keeping the body tense through
the endless hours, the corpse is taken

back to base and all blood ends in water. It is
the bird unseen takes a spent heart to ocean

At the farthest point in space-time,
at the greatest point of geographical distance
into proposed adventure—
from which only return was possible,
doubling back over our tracks—
there was no paint, no color,
the bare planks only for a habitation.
Here colorless death could have its way
and be hardly noticed. Here even
green paled, as if polluted
by the bare planks. People were disappeared
shaking their heads at this disaster,
as bodiless as ghosts silently threading
brotherhood bracelets over my wrist

Think now as if the forest's parts were clouds
meshing with each other, some dark, some
light, or lighter. The green mass has the name
duration: one tree replacing another and never
falling but of its own accord and in obedience
to the common law. Nothing despoiled,
nothing torn down, nothing cut in its very life
leaving its blood over the jungle floor.
Clouds billowing but contained in the mass
although some, like balloons, could seem to
take off—if looked at long and hard enough.
Up there in the wails, on invisible paths,
leeches immeasurably patient below leaves,
bodies gyrating to warmth of mammal flesh

And, at the end, the forest closes in
on itself, and stops to admire itself, and
rests. Astounded at its own beauty
it gives assent to the planet
that it should continue, that it should
survive and its ark of creatures also.
This is where the birds
have become color
against a relentless green.
Across the mass of tints
white undulation headed with black,
Terpsiphone a! paradisi,
deserves the appellation heaven.
In the middle of the scene
the vast river hushes too, rapt in its
rapids, its bridal veils of water,
creating a sound recognized as distance.
Far from the world of corporations
in murderous contention, the forest wonders
how men will last. Sun falls on leaves
a blessing lighting their myriad veins: it is
as if the air itself were sung with joy
in the temperate heat of earliest morning:
day is as light as a young hero, not
yet weighing on banks in suffocation

At the back of all buildings in the cities
mocking parameters of "progress"
forest walls rise in abundance and from
the walls hang the great war cloths
along whose strands the race depends.

All beings once woven into the cloths,
all beings compete there for air to breathe
and food with which to tamp their hunger.
The early patterns are the most complex
with the hooks on which creation hangs,
all hangs together in a famous peace
between the warring tribes of the great currents,
set many years before in a red-dye bath:
back when an emperor lost out at Waterloo.
This archaic image of the golden births
which the tribe looks back to as its hair
tears from the hooks holding the heads
in place: enemy heads ferociously parted
from neighbor bodies, together with
its own vivid catastrophes. But heads
are not taken anymore—only the honors won
by suffocating those who are too poor
to eat their forest any longer, die in the ghastly
cities, imbecile jobs. The stench of sewers open
for all to smell and drop into with both feet clawing
as they fall from the great cloths of their lives

Conjunction of forest and sea
dark crimson dragonfly linking the two
stitching together landscapes of the mind
where we have seen before, head above
clouds, landscapes remembered from another
life, remembered by each other. Too much
diversity hiding the forest's own
behind a mask of sameness. I won't
say "previous," would rather claim
some simultaneous lives running parallel,

with trigger hairs from time to time
between them. Steadfastly birds
refuse to manifest: they fly the gardens
far below this perch. I climbed this
mountain by mistake on a bitch trail.
No matter for my mind is so replete with birds,
so fabulous a kingdom of the upper sky
cannot be abdicated for a bunch of facts,
a bunch of species ticked off in a book:
I am content behind these empty eyes.
The dragonfly has left for the far mountain
opposite, the beach's other shore. I shall
go down as well, my time goes down
the joyous sky and drinks drink up each
other. I am as thirsty at this water as if this
were my desert. The sun begets a second star

What if this butterfly
is the color of sky and night
and this one of the sea and night
and this one in the sun's blaze
at midnight on the alternate side
of world—night being the high color
of wing and day being the low?
I should have been a butterfly-watcher
for they are out in the open
with their delicate touches of paint
in the midst of horror—whereas
the birds now, the birds alas...
Butterflies are more direct
with their shorter spans more patient,
read out to me in wavering lines

brief life and its annihilation.
Whereas the birds move on and on,
pierce the sky like arrows, never seem to fall.
Their death is a quiet one in the deep forest
as the death of the forest is not quiet:
the towering trees fall over and over.
One dusk, as the light went down over the river,
the one bird I had dreamed of seeing and despaired
of ever seeing as the days went by, finally
Lord *Buceros* himself, prince of forest and sky,
bird of the river gods and gods of fallen heads,
dropped out of the sky and covered a tree
and seemed as large as the tree, covering it entirely.
It was still possible to glimpse the colors of the head
and know it for itself. Although this bright darkness
preceded the death, a death mourned by its fellows,
warrior-bird was known: for me, a death redeemed

Lem Baa; Sungai Kinabatangan, Sabah; Miri, Mulu,
Batang Baram; Sungai Pelutan; Sibu, Kapit, Kai Wong/Pala Wong, Batang
Rajang; Kuching, Kubah, Bako, Sungai Santubong /
Sungai Sarawak, 2005

Note

"Ins and Outs of the Forest Rivers" arose out of, and was written during, two months' travel in the wild regions of Sarawak, Borneo, East Malaysia, in 2005. Anthropological and archaeological interests were fed by visits to contemporary indigenous settlements and historic sites; other interests by, for example, bird-watching in the Kinabatangan River area of Sabah and a number of national parks.

   I was given a once-in-a-lifetime opportunity to volunteer as an anthropologist with people who were trying to help indigenous communities find alternative lifeways after losing lands to logging, oil palm plantations, etc. There was to be an eighteen-day tour to a variety of communities, including settled and still-migratory forest folk, and a conference of elders from such tribal backgrounds. The travel was very rough for me, approaching age 80.

   On the fourth night, at the furthest geographical point of the tour (from which backtracking would be necessary), after inspecting new gardens and after discussions at a village meeting, my colleague/guide and I slept on the floor of the headman's house. In the morning, this colleague was found dead of a heart attack. It took some eighteen hours to get the body back to base, and it was another three days until the funeral. After this, all plans were changed. The privacy of individuals and locations has been respected in the poem.